Joseph the Dreamer

Joseph the

by Shoshana Lepon

Illustrated by Aaron Friedman

 The Judaica Press • 1991 • New York

Dreamer

הנה בעל החלמות ... ונראה מה יהיו חלמתיו

"Here comes the dreamer ... let us see what will become of his dreams!" (Genesis 37:19, 20)

Dedicated to the children of
The Diaspora Yeshiva Day School
Mt. Zion, Israel

A special thanks

To my parents, Dr. and Mrs. David Loev and Carl and Pat Lepon

To Rabbi and Rebbitzen Mordechai Goldstein, shlita, of Diaspora Yeshiva

To Yeshara Gold and Rabbi Daniel Isaacs for their insightful comments

And to my husband for his constant support

ABOUT THE AUTHOR

Shoshana Lepon teaches advanced Judaic studies at the Diaspora Yeshiva Women's Seminary in the Old City of Jerusalem. She lives on Mt. Zion, adjacent to the site of King David's Tomb, with her husband, a teacher of Talmud, and their children. Mrs. Lepon is the author of a number of children's books, including *The Ten Tests of Abraham* and *The Ten Plagues of Egypt*, both published by the Judaica Press, Inc.

ABOUT THE ILLUSTRATOR

Aaron Friedman has illustrated the works of many Jewish authors and has contributed frequently to various widely read magazines. His pictures can be seen also in *The Ten Plagues of Egypt*.

© Copyright 1991
THE JUDAICA PRESS, INC.
Brooklyn, NY

Library of Congress Catalog Card No. 90-091925 √
ISBN: 0-910818-92-4 Hardcover edition
ISBN: 0-910818-93-2 Softcover edition

Printed in Singapore

Jacob had twelve boys
And he loved each one
But Joseph the dreamer
Was his favorite son.

So Jacob gave Joseph
A striped coat to wear.
His brothers grew jealous—
It didn't seem fair!

5

But what angered them more
Than this colorful cloak
Were the two boastful dreams
Of which young Joseph spoke:

"In the field we were stacking
Our sheaves on the ground
When mine stood upright
And yours knelt, all around.

"Eleven bright stars
And the moon and the sun
All bowed down before me,
The powerful one."

They pulled off the coat
That had started the split
And threw Joseph into
A deep rocky pit.

Said his brothers, "This means
That what you'd like to do
Is to rule over all of us—
Our parents, too!

"Do you think we would crown
Such a young one as king?
We'd have to be fools
To do such a thing!"

7

Joseph was trapped!
He could not get free.
But in G-d's hidden plan
It was all meant to be.

The sons went to their flock
And killed a young goat;
They sprinkled its blood
On their brother's striped coat.

Then they brought it to Jacob
And said, "Come and see
This torn bloody coat.
Now whose could it be?"

"That coat is Joseph's!"
Their poor father cried,
"A beast has attacked him.
He surely has died!"

Jacob tore at his clothes,
And put dust on his head
He cried many days
Thinking Joseph was dead.

But Joseph still lived—
As his brothers knew well.
They kept it a secret
And no one would tell.

9

They thought they would never
See Joseph again,
For they'd sold their brother
To traveling men.

Those men went to Egypt
To the great slave bazaar,
And there they sold Joseph
To Sir Potiphar.

Joseph was faithful
And honest and wise.
He proved himself worthy
In his master's eyes.

10

So Potiphar said,
"Run my household for me!"
In G-d's hidden plan
It was all meant to be.

Joseph worked hard
In Potiphar's home,
But his master's wife
Would not leave him alone.

She followed behind him
And called, "Stay with me!"
But Joseph was strong;
He would never agree!

11

"How could I spend time
With another man's wife?
Before I'd do that
I would give up my life!"

He ran off, leaving
His cloak on the scene.
And then she decided
To do something mean.

"This slave tried to hurt me!"
She pointed him out.
"He crept up behind me ...
I started to shout ...

When Potiphar saw
That she held Joseph's cloak
He accepted the lies
That his sneaky wife spoke.

"I yelled for my guards
And he ran off in fear.
But his cloak fell behind.
Look! I have it right here!"

Into jail he threw Joseph,
Behind lock and key.
But in G-d's hidden plan
It was all meant to be.

Joseph sat for ten years
In that dungeon of stone
He prayed G-d would free him
And let him go home.

Pharaoh sent his baker
And butler to jail
For a rock in his bread
And a fly in his ale.

They told Joseph their dreams
And the butler spoke first:
"Three grape vines I squeezed
To quench Pharaoh's thirst."

14

"In three days," said Joseph,
"Everything will be fine.
You'll return to the palace
To pour Pharaoh's wine."

Said the baker, "I dreamed
Of three baskets of bread.
But birds came and stole them
Right off of my head."

"In three days," said Joseph,
"I'm afraid, you'll be dead—
Someone else will be chosen
To bake Pharaoh's bread."

15

So Joseph explained it.
And as he'd predicted
The butler was freed
And the baker convicted.

Two more years had to pass
Before Joseph went free.
But in G-d's hidden plan
It was all meant to be.

Pharaoh had two dreams
That woke him one night.
He jumped from his bed;
He was trembling with fright.

He had seen seven cows
That were healthy and chubby
Eaten by seven cows
Skinny and grubby.

And then seven ears
Of corn, good and sweet,
Were swallowed by seven
Too dried up to eat.

Pharaoh called to his wise men:
"Explain this to me!"
But none of them knew
What the meaning could be.

17

Then the butler spoke up:
"There's a young man in jail
Who understands dreams,
Each one without fail!"

"Bring him at once!"
Pharaoh cried, "Bring him here!
I'll have no peace
'Til these dreams become clear."

Joseph was taken
Right out of the jail.
He heard the strange dreams
And explained each detail:

18

"G-d sent a warning
In the dreams that you had—
There will be seven good years
And then seven bad.

"You must save up food
From every year's crop,
Before all the good years
Come to a stop."

"You're so wise!" marveled Pharaoh.
"You shall rule under me!"
In G-d's hidden plan
It was all meant to be.

19

Pharaoh passed a new law,
And he sent a command
To all of the farmers
Who worked Egypt's land.

"Pack up your wheat
Your barley, your hay
And bring it to Joseph
Who will store it away."

Joseph, seven years later,
Controlled Egypt's bread.
Everyone served him
And did as he said.

But back home in Canaan
There was no food to eat.
Jacob ordered his sons:
"Go to Egypt for wheat!"

To the palace they came,
To the second-in-power.
Bowing low to the ground,
They asked to buy flour.

This great prince was Joseph
Though none of them knew.
His brothers were bowing.
The dreams had come true!

21

But Joseph behaved
As though he were a stranger.
He cried, "You are spies!
You will put us in danger."

"Oh no! We're just ten
Of twelve sons," they replied.
"The youngest is home,
And one is lost—or has died."

"Then bring me the youngest,
To prove there's another."
To make sure they'd return
Joseph kept back one brother.

22

In their sacks they discovered
All the money they'd paid.
They showed Jacob the bundles;
They all were afraid.

"I have now lost two sons.
You ask a third one from me?
I will go to the grave
From so much misery!"

The sons begged their father
But he only said "No!"
He refused to agree
That his young one should go.

23

But their food soon ran out
And the famine was strong;
So the sons were sent back
With the youngest along.

When Joseph saw Benjamin
He hid tears of joy;
He had not seen this brother
Since he'd been a small boy.

They were seated at tables
In his royal hall.
But still Joseph pretended
Not to know them at all.

The sons started home,
But were searched on the way.
The cup was discovered—
Now what could they say?

For he wished to teach them
The great wrong they had done
In causing their father
To grieve for his son.

So Joseph took grain
And filled each man's sack.
Then he hid his own cup
In Benjamin's pack.

They came before Joseph
Humbled and shaken.
"The young one must serve me
For what he has taken!"

"We cannot cause our father
More pain!" was their cry.
"If he loses *this* son,
He surely will die!"

Now Joseph could not
Hide himself anymore;
He sent out his servants
And bolted the door.

"I'm Joseph!" he cried out,
"The brother you sold!
Bring me my father
Who must be so old.

"Bring your wives,
    bring your children
And live here with me!"
In G-d's hidden plan
It was all meant to be.

The brothers were speechless.
They knew they'd done wrong.
Yet Joseph still loved them
And had all along:

27

They rushed home with the news
For their father to hear:
"Joseph still lives
After twenty-two years!"

Their families gathered,
The big and the small.
They numbered seventy
People in all.

They climbed into wagons
The fathers, the mothers
The nieces, the nephews,
The sisters, the brothers.

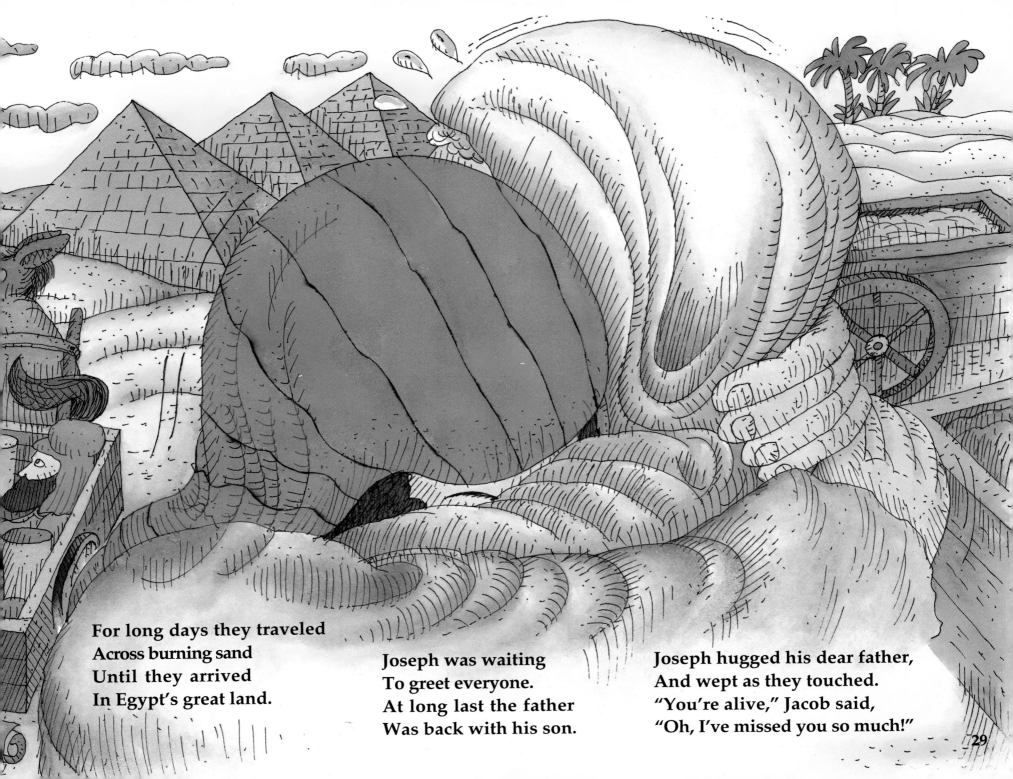

For long days they traveled
Across burning sand
Until they arrived
In Egypt's great land.

Joseph was waiting
To greet everyone.
At long last the father
Was back with his son.

Joseph hugged his dear father,
And wept as they touched.
"You're alive," Jacob said,
"Oh, I've missed you so much!"

The brothers grew still.
They were filled with great shame.
Their father had suffered
And they were to blame.

"Do not feel so bad,"
Whispered Joseph, "you see,
In G-d's hidden plan,
It was all meant to be!"

TOPICS FOR DISCUSSION

1) In the dreams, what did these things represent?
   a] twelve sheaves of straw; b] eleven stars, the sun, and the moon;
   c] three clusters of grapes; d] three baskets of bread;
   e] seven healthy cows; f] seven sickly cows;
   g] seven good ears of corn; h] seven dry ears of corn.

2) What good came from Joseph's stay in jail?

3) How did Joseph become so powerful?

4) How did Joseph teach his brothers that they had done wrong?

5) When did Joseph believe that his brothers understood the pain they had caused their father?

6) How did the brothers realize that Joseph loved them and did not blame them for their actions?

7) How did Joseph comfort his brothers when they felt ashamed of what they had done?

8) How did Joseph's stay in Egypt benefit his entire family?

DID YOU KNOW...?

Joseph was so handsome that the Egyptian women would climb upon the city walls to look at him. When he walked by, they would throw their jewelry at him to get his attention. *(Midrash Rabbah)*

Joseph knew a special way to keep Egypt's food fresh. He packed each type of food with some of the earth from the place where it had grown, and this kept it from spoiling for many years. *(Rashi)*

Joseph proved his identity by telling his brothers that they had sold him. No one else knew this, because they all had kept the secret. *(Sforno)*

The sons were afraid to tell Jacob that Joseph was alive. They worried that the shock would kill him. They asked Asher's daughter, Serach, to

play her harp for her grandfather and sing, "Joseph still lives, Joseph still lives...." In this gentle way Jacob learned the good news. *(Meam Loez)*

The famine stopped after only two years instead of seven, because when Jacob came to Egypt he brought a blessing with him. After Jacob died, the famine began again. *(Ramban)*

Many of the things that happened to Joseph had happened to his father Jacob, as well. Jacob's brother, Esav, made trouble for him, and Joseph's brothers made trouble for him; both had to leave their homes and live far away; both were separated from their parents for twenty-two years; both started out with nothing and became rich. And both had important dreams.

(Midrash Rabbah)